BEI GRIN MACHT SICH II
WISSEN BEZAHLT

- Wir veröffentlichen Ihre Hausarbeit,
  Bachelor- und Masterarbeit

- Ihr eigenes eBook und Buch -
  weltweit in allen wichtigen Shops

- Verdienen Sie an jedem Verkauf

Jetzt bei www.GRIN.com hochladen und kostenlos publizieren

Bibliographic information published by the German National Library:

The German National Library lists this publication in the National Bibliography; detailed bibliographic data are available on the Internet at http://dnb.dnb.de .

Imprint:

Copyright © 2018 GRIN Verlag
Print and binding: Books on Demand GmbH, Norderstedt Germany
ISBN: 9783668913219

This book at GRIN:

https://www.grin.com/document/459581

Oguzhan Bekar

Aus der Reihe: e-fellows.net stipendiaten-wissen

e-fellows.net (Hrsg.)

Band 3062

Artificial Intelligence. Benefits, Risks and Effects on Society

GRIN Verlag

GRIN - Your knowledge has value

Since its foundation in 1998, GRIN has specialized in publishing academic texts by students, college teachers and other academics as e-book and printed book. The website www.grin.com is an ideal platform for presenting term papers, final papers, scientific essays, dissertations and specialist books.

Visit us on the internet:

http://www.grin.com/

http://www.facebook.com/grincom

http://www.twitter.com/grin_com

Bachelorarbeit

zur Erlangung des Grades eines **Bachelor of Science** an der Volkswirtschaftlichen Fakultät der

Ludwig-Maximilians-Universität zu München

Titel:

"Artificial Intelligence: Benefits, Risks and Effects on Society"

.

München,
den 06. August 2018

Eingereicht von:
Oguzhan Hilmi Bekar

Contents

1 Introduction

AI has been a buzzword since its beginning in the late 1950s. However, the recent robust and developing focus on four self-enforcing trends take the notion of disruptive technologies onto a higher level. These are statistical and probabilistic methods, the abundance of increasingly large amounts of data, the accessibility of cheap, enormous computational power, and the transformation and adaption of more places into IT-friendly environments (e.g., Smart Cities and IoT).

These fundamental elements of AI can be found in many applications. Boston Consulting Group (2017) states some of these applications as follows: Marketing and Sales with personalized services and goods, Research and Development with aggressive forms of data collection and automating previously outsourced service tasks in large companies by combining AI with robotic processing automation[1].

AI's unprecedented ubiquity among these areas and more has underlined the feasibility, importance, and scalability of AI. Consequently, critical voices raised about how this enormous disruptive technology should be regulated and adjusted into the economy. As a response to the ethical, social and economic impact of AI, in October 2016, the White House Office of Science and Technology Policy (OSTP), the European Parliament's Committee on Legal Affairs, and in the UK, the House of Commons' Science and Technology Committee released their initial reports on how to prepare for the future of AI.

Furthermore, in contrast to the presumptions about the adverse effects of AI on wages and employment, which had led the discussion into a false dichotomy, this paper introduces a more distinguished analysis. In the final analysis, the authors suggest that AI reduces wages and demand for jobs which can be replaced by AI. However, and this is the missing element causing the false dichotomy, Artificial Intelligence and automation induce countervailing effects which increase the demand for traditional non-automated tasks. Also, AI helps to create new labor-intensive tasks which in turn increase labor share and thereby counterbalance the displacement effect of automation in the aggregate.

Nevertheless, automation decreased wages and amount of jobs for low-skill and medium-skill occupations and caused an increased inequality and employment polarization. (e.g., Autor et al. (2003), Goos and Manning (2007), Michaels et al. (2014)). The IFR estimates that current industrial robots operations amount to 1.5-1.75 million, while Boston Consulting Group (2015) states that this figure could go up to 4-6 million by 2025 in the U.S.

Although automation is abundant, yet, it seems unlikely that we know much about the impact of technologies, especially of robots, on the society. Nonetheless, there are estimations about the scale of AI's impact. Based on the tasks employed, over the next two decades, Frey and Osborne (2017) estimate that 47% of US workers are at risk while McKinsey (2017) estimates the number at 45%.

---

[1]Observing the worker's performance and learning by repeating the steps successively to automate the tasks.

Albeit these incredibly high numbers, there is no guarantee that firms will effectively automate. According to the profit maximization calculation, they would only automate if it is beneficial to substitute machines for labor and consider how much wages change in response to this threat.

Moreover, not only the place of automation is decisive, but also how other sectors and occupations react to it. It could be that other industries soak up the freed workers, or even automated industries could expand employment due to higher productivity.

Going beyond speculative figures mentioned above, Acemoglu and Restrepo (2017) estimate the equilibrium impact of one type of automation technology: Industrial robot: "an automatically controlled, reprogrammable, and multipurpose machine." Most closely to this work is the paper by Graetz and Michaels (2015). Their work variates the data across industries in different countries and estimates that industrial robots increase productivity and wages while the employment of low-skill workers decreases. The data used in Acemoglu and Restrepo (2017) and the above-mentioned paper use are the same, but the empirical method variates and allows Acemoglu and Restrepo to observe cross-country, cross-industry comparisons, exploit exogenous changes in the spread of robots, and estimate the equilibrium impact of robots on local labor markets. The Micro-data mentioned above also allows them to control for detailed demographic and compositional variables when focusing on commuting zones and study the impact of robots on industry and occupation-level outcomes.

This thesis provides a framework to think about AI and how it affects and shapes the society. The primary references used are as follows:

- Acemoglu and Restrepo (2018)

- Acemoglu and Restrepo (2017)

- Cath et al. (2018)

Finally, this thesis is structured as follows. First I will start summarizing the Theoretical and Empirical Approaches by Acemoglu and Restrepo in stating the effects of Automation on wages and employment. Afterward, I will state Cath et al.'s review of recent policymaking decisions regarding AI and how to "make a Good AI Society" by the U.S., EU and UK. Furthermore, after each section, I am going to discuss each paper respectively and supplement them with my findings. Finally, I will state further novel research which could foster implementing a society in which AI does more help than harm and conclude afterward.

2 Methodology

In this section, I will respectively summarize two papers with a theoretical and empirical approach. The theoretical paper: "Artificial Intelligence, Automation and Work" and the empirical paper: "Robots and Jobs: Evidence from US labor markets" by Acemoglu and Restrepo (2018) and Acemoglu and Restrepo (2017) respectively. While the former provides insights into the implications of both Artificial Intelligence and Automation, the latter one focuses on Industrial Robots. The reason for choosing different technological focal points is that there was no other recent empirical data regarding the effects of Artificial Intelligence on wages or employment. Although acknowledging the technological differences between Artificial Intelligence and Industrial Robots, I nonetheless consider these both technologies to be similar concerning economic and societal implications as we shall see in this section.

2.1 Theoretical Approach

In this section, I summarize the findings of Acemoglu and Restrepo (2018). The following subsection is structured as follows: After introducing and explaining the occurring effects of AI to revisit the dichotomy verbally, I will afterward present the formal implications.

2.1.1 Countervailing Effects

Productivity Effect: Reduces the cost of production and thereby increases the demand for labor in non-automated tasks. As cheaper capital substitutes for labor in specific tasks, the prices of the goods and services will decrease and make the households effectively wealthier which ultimately increases the demand for such goods and services. There are two complementary ways through which the Productivity Effect works.

The first point is *labor demand* which might expand in the same sectors undergoing automation by reinstating workers in tasks which can't be automated by AI. This is epitomized by the rapid spread of ATMs (Automated Teller Machines). ATM as a new technology displaced bank tellers which were more expensive for the banks. However, at the same time banks were enabled to open more branches as costs sharply fell and consequently employ more bank tellers who did jobs which ATMs could not automate Bessen (2015).

Secondly, AI causes higher real incomes by reducing the cost of production and consequently the price of consumption. This, in turn, causes higher demand for all products which triggers a higher demand for labor in other industries due to the increased supply of goods. Exemplary is the mechanization of the agriculture. Due to lower food prices, mechanization enriched consumers who then demanded more non-agricultural goods as suggested by Herrendorf et al. (2013). These examples reveal a crucial implication of automation as stated in (e.g.,Brynjolfsson and McAfee (2014)). The danger, thus lower wages, and higher unemployment seem not to be resulting from highly productive technologies which affect other industries positively, but rather from mediocre technologies which are barely productive enough to be adopted, hence cause displacement.

Capital Accumulation: Arises from the fact that automation binds high capital (Allen (2009), Olmstead and Rhode (2001)). The high demand for capital triggers all the

3

more capital accumulation, for instance by increasing the rental rate of capital. The higher capital, in turn, raises the demand for labor.

Deepening of Automation: Different from the former described Productivity Effect which affects the jobs extensively[2] and thereby displaces workers, here the intensively deepening of automation instead raises from within the productivity of already automated tasks without causing the loss of jobs.

An illustrative example of this can be found in the replacement of horse-powered reapers and harvesters by diesel tractors (Olmstead and Rhode (2001); Manuelli and Seshadri (2014)).

All in all, these countervailing effects reveal, that the displacement effect by automation is not necessarily accurate in all scenarios. Disruptive technologies affect workers in two respects: While some abolished tasks can cause the workers to be unemployed in one sector, other sectors could be triggered to raise their demands for new labor arising from the increased productivity and higher real incomes.

However, one effect of automation cannot be counteracted upon: The increasing substitution of capital for labor which lowers the share of labor in national income. The tasks, the labor will execute, could be shredded down to a smaller set. Nevertheless, the ever-existing automation in history has yet to exhibit a decline in the share of labor in national income. The following headline New Tasks suggest the reason why we did not see such a development.

New Tasks: Historically, periods of intensive automation were always accompanied by the creation of new job descriptions. For instance, Acemoglu and Restrepo (2016) find that between 1980 and 2010, half of the employment growth in the USA resulted from the creation of new job titles. Acemoglu and Restrepo refer to this as the Reinstatement Effect, which creates new tasks to oppose the Displacement Effect, and thus can lead to a balanced growth path.

AI could help to create new tasks in two ways, as emphasized by this paper. Rapid automation may endogenously generate the incentive to establish new labor-intensive tasks. Such that if automation goes ahead of new tasks, the wages will decrease and further automation is less profitable. So, the firm will profit more if it introduces new labor-intensive tasks.

Moreover, Automation Technology Platforms such as AI could create new tasks. Future job descriptions could be called "AI Trainers, AI Explainers, and AI Sustainers" (Accenture PLC).

Finally, AI could be applied to enable the individual education for disabled students so they can take part in community life on equal terms. A policy Germany wants to establish in the form of an inclusive education system Werning (2014).

---

[2]The word 'extensive' indicates that the new technology is unrelated to the old one, thus is considered exogenous, while 'intensive' means that old technologies are being improved.

2.1.2 Impeding Effects

The above-described effects so far explained how the negative aspects of AI could be counterbalanced, at least in theory. In practice, however, ensuring the smooth transition of reinstating displaced workers can be a tricky endeavor.

Firstly, Acemoglu and Restrepo are pointing to the changes like existing jobs. The process enhances both that workers find new jobs and learn the needed skills. New tasks tend to require new skills. If the education system cannot provide the necessary skills, the adjustment of new technologies can be hampered. Deloitte suggests that if specific technologies need a parallel execution by human beings, the lack of the necessary skills will impede the potential productivity outcomes of such technologies. Therefore, introductions of new technologies need time to exhibit positive effects on the economy. Before wages and labor demand can increase, wages could stagnate, poverty expand, and living conditions worsened.

Intimately connected to the first point, the second argument concerns the excessive automation, meaning faster automation than socially desirable. As a result, excessive automation creates inefficiencies by wasting resources and displacing labor and thereby impeding the transition process Acemoglu and Restrepo (2018).

2.1.3 The Basic Formal Model

The basic model introduced in this paper is the simple model of a task-based framework used in Acemoglu and Restrepo (2016). In contrast to a standard aggregated production function, T1 considers tasks as the central unit of production, instead of a good or service such that

$$\ln Y = \int_{N-1}^{N} \ln y(x) \, dx. \tag{T1}$$

where Y denotes aggregate output, and y(x) is the output of task x. The tasks run only from N-1 to N so that we can examine new tasks without changing the whole aggregate.

Each task can either be executed by human labor l(x) or machines m(x), depending on whether the task has been technologically automated or not. The output of task x

$$y(x) = \begin{cases} \gamma_L(x)\,\ell(x) + \gamma_M(x)\,m(x) & if\ x \in [0, I] \\ \gamma_L(x)\,\ell(x) & if\ x \in (I, N] \end{cases} \tag{T2}$$

considers all $x \in [0, I]$ to be automated, thus to be executed by either machines or labor depending on the productivity γ_M and γ_L respectively. I denotes the threshold of tasks which can be automated with current technological knowledge and the range $x \in (I, N]$

those ones which cannot. Hence, the upper function of $y_L(x)$ is the output of both labor and machines while the lower function states the output by labor only. Furthermore, a realistic representation of human-machine relationship is considered in the assumption that $\gamma_L(x)/\gamma_M(x)$ increases in x. The given intuition here is that labor has a learning curve with an upward slope, whereas on the other side machines are considered to have a constant learning curve without marginal gains. Hence, implying that labor has a comparative advantage over machines in higher indexed tasks. Moreover, it suggests consistency when looking at the assumption that only human labor can execute tasks in the higher ranges, namely $x \in (I, N]$.

The demand for labor can be expressed as a function of Wage ($W =$ the marginal product of labor) equaling labor $(N - 1)$ times the exponent of labor in the aggregate production function as follows

$$W = (N - I)\frac{Y}{L}. \tag{T3}$$

Transforming the equation we receive the share of labor in national income

$$s_L = \frac{WL}{Y} = N - I. \tag{T4}$$

Both equations decrease in I, indicating that by increasing automation wages and consequently the share of labor in national income declines.

2.1.4 Technology and Labor Demand

Following types of technological change induce different kinds of effects on employment.

- (Extensive) Automation expands the set of automated tasks represented by I
- Labor-augmenting technological advances increase $\gamma_L(x)$
- (Intensive) Deepening of automation increases $\gamma_M(x)$ for $x \leq I$[3]
- Creation of new tasks increases the tasks (N) in which labor has a comparative advantage over machines

While the last three technological changes do not necessarily displace labor, the first one exhibits a direct displacement effect, per results of this paper. To show how the displacement, arising from new technologies, is counteracted I will now state formally the countervailing effects.

Examining formally, one can see two opposing implications when automating a task as follows.

---

[3]The assumption is that $\gamma_M(x) = \gamma_M$ for all x. Thus, the Deepening of automation tends to increase labor demand and wages instead of displacing labor.

$$\frac{\mathrm{d}\ln W}{\mathrm{d}I} = \underbrace{-\frac{1}{N-I}}_{\text{Displacement effect} < 0} + \underbrace{\ln\left(\frac{W}{\gamma_L(I)}\right) - \ln\left(\frac{R}{\gamma_M(I)}\right)}_{\text{Productivity effect} > 0}. \tag{T5}$$

The Productivity Effect increases both the demand for labor where automation is taking place and in other industries where automation is not that prevalent. Both effects sum up to the productivity effect seen in T5. However, if the productivity effect is limited, automation will always reduce labor demand.

This equation implies that if new technologies are only productive enough to replace one specific task but not highly productive enough to impact other tasks within an industry positively, these "so-so" technologies will exhibit displacement effects.

Formally, one can see that when $\gamma_{M/R} = \gamma_{L/W}$, the "so-so" techs will have a displacement effect. If on the other hand, $\gamma_{M/R} > \gamma_{L/W}$, the productivity is sufficient to raise the demand for labor and wages. This is consistent with the hypothesis that only technologies which reveal comparative advantages over traditional labor will be applied.

However, the derivative of T4

$$\frac{\mathrm{d}s_L}{\mathrm{d}I} = -1 < 0 \tag{T6}$$

shows that regardless of the productivity, the share of labor in national income will always decline, because automation always increases the productivity more than the wages[4].

Apart from the Productivity Effect, there are two other counteracting forces, as already mentioned in Section 2.1.1, which rather mitigate the displacement effect by affecting the Productivity of the new technology.

Capital Accumulation: Acemoglu and Restrepo (2018) initially assumed that the supply of capital is fixed, such that investments in new machines increase the demand for capital and thus increase the rental rate R. The other more realistic possibility is that the newly bought machines do have a positive impact on the costs of production. And thus, as machines and labor are complements, an increase in the capital stock with a constant share of labor will rather increase the wages and reduce the rental rate. The productivity effect is as a result of this even more significant, as can be seen in T5.

Interestingly, however, T4 still applies and continues to decrease the share of labor in national income. The intuition is again that the productivity gain arising from automation is always higher than the increase in wages.

Deepening of Automation: A further powerful effect is the improvement of already automated tasks which doesn't make the worker obsolete but slightly increases its produc-

---

[4] $\mathrm{d}\ln(Y/L)/\mathrm{d}I > \mathrm{d}\ln W/\mathrm{d}I$, as inferred from T5.

tivity. Translated into the model, this would mean an increase of $\gamma_M(x)$ for tasks $x \leq I$. If we further assume that $\gamma_M(x) = \gamma_M$ (for all x)[5], we can conclude that the Deepening of Automation tends to increase the labor demand and wages as stated by the total derivative of wage

$$\mathrm{d}\ln W / \mathrm{d}\ln Y / L = (I - N + 1)\mathrm{d}\ln \gamma_M > 0.$$

New tasks and the share of labor: More potent than the countervailing forces is the establishment of new tasks in which the labor has a comparative advantage over machines. In the formal perspective, this would translate into an increase of the set of tasks (N) as follows

$$\frac{\mathrm{d}\ln W}{\mathrm{d}N} = \underbrace{\ln\left(\frac{R}{\gamma_M(N-1)}\right) - \ln\left(\frac{W}{\gamma_L(N)}\right)}_{\text{Productivity effect} > 0} + \underbrace{\frac{1}{N-1}}_{\text{Reinstatement effect} > 0} . \tag{T7}$$

In contrast to the effects as mentioned above, T7 reveals that the increase in new tasks does not induce a displacement effect. Instead, we can see two effects going in the same direction, namely the positive effects of Productivity and Reinstatement. Moreover, we can also see that the share of labor in national income does indeed increase as such

$$\frac{\mathrm{d}s_L}{\mathrm{d}N} = 1.$$

This is intuitive because the share of labor increases by new tasks: I has to grow the same amount as N, then and only then equilibrium wages grow proportionately with productivity and the labor share s_L remains constant.

Mismatch of new technologies and skills and Inequality: Even if there are newly established and applied tasks, there is still a potential mismatch between the required skills of the workforce and the requirement of the new technologies or tasks. Let's consider the following parameters in the next model – For brevity, I will only state equations for comparative reasons. Full values can be looked upon the Online Appendix:

L: Low skill supply H: High skill supply;
L can only perform $S \in (I, N)$ while H can perform all tasks: $H \in [0, N]$.

Hence, while low skill workers will earn a wage of W_L, high skill workers will earn a wage of $W_H \geq W_L$.

Higher S implies that there are plenty of tasks the low skilled employees can perform, while a lower S implies that there are only a few tasks left that low-skilled workers can perform. Thus, $N - S$ can be seen as the mismatch.

---

[5] Assuming that for different figures of task indexes the marginal productivity does not change.

Hence, the impact of automation on inequality is the wage premium between high and low skilled workers.

$$\frac{\mathrm{d}\ln W_H/W_L}{\mathrm{d}I} = \frac{1}{S-I} > 0.$$

This inequality shows that the wage premium increases in I. In other words, the wage gap increases when the non-automated set of tasks decreases. This is intuitive because if S is close to I, the low skilled workers will be squeezed into only a small range of tasks which they can perform. This will lead to decreasing wages as the supply of workers will concentrate on the small number of left jobs. If S is big, however, the low skilled workers will have a more extensive set of tasks to perform and consequently won't concentrate on one particular small set of tasks. This raises an interesting point mentioned before in the text: If automation does not go hand in hand with new job descriptions, the share of labor or low-skilled workers in national income will shrink.

Besides that, equally important are the implications of a mismatch for the productivity gains from new tasks: If $\frac{W_H}{R}$ is relatively high, or S is relatively low, the productivity gains from new tasks will be limited. This happens because new tasks require high-skill workers who are scarce and expensive when S is low and R is nearly constant.

$$\frac{W_H}{R} = \frac{N-S}{I-N+1}\frac{K}{L}$$

In order to prevent inequality due to automation, decision-makers need to foster an environment in which the supply of skills goes hand in hand with new technologies. See for this policy-making in Section 4.

2.1.5 Discussion

Impeding effects slow down the transition process and reveal a conflict of objective between encouraging the workforce to acquire specific skills in AI and excessively investing in this specific technology. On the one hand, to solve the first point, we want to accelerate the learning process by concentrating the resources on Artificial Intelligence. On the other hand, we see that excessively using these resources for one specific technology causes inefficiencies.

Acemoglu and Restrepo (2018) try to find an equilibrium model concerning the grade of Artificial Intelligence and the effects on employment and wages, as we saw in the formal section. The above-described conflict of objective could be solved when the optimal intensity of resources for the development of AI could be found. The inefficiently used resources, on the other hand, could then be used for different technologies in order to mitigate the short-term adverse effects of displacement by creating tasks unrelated to AI, making the transition process smoother.

The problem with the current discussion in new technologies and labor is that the discourse fails to anticipate the balance between automation and the creation of new tasks.

9

However, AI could indeed disturb this balance by causing the automation to grow faster than the creation of new tasks, also because the adjustment of new tasks to automation is a slow process. Therefore, an education system needs to keep up with the demand for new skills. How opaque the future might seem from today's perspective; one thing is sure: The market becomes increasingly disruptive and requires human capital to be flexible and ready to educate oneself continuously. Yuval Harari exemplifies this intuition as follows:

> "[...] in 1017, poor Chinese parents taught their children how to plant rice or weave silk, and wealthier parents taught their boys how to read and write or to fight on horseback, and their girls to be modest and obedient housewives. It was obvious that these skills would still be needed. In 2017, by contrast, we have no such certainties about the future of jobs, gender, economics or even death" Harari (2017).

Besides that, for $\gamma_L(x)/\gamma_M(x)$ to increase, the authors have assumed that machines cannot learn over time. However, when precisely thinking about technological potentials of AI, one can predict that this assumption does not hold anymore. On the contrary, prospects of Thrun and Pratt (2012) about Machine Learning suggest that we are on the edge of revolutionizing the notion that robots have to be re-programmed by humans when adjusting for different tasks.

2.2 Empirical Approach

In this subsection, I will review significant parts of the paper of Acemoglu and Restrepo (2017) by stating its empirical evidence on the effects of automation on wages and employment.

This review is structured as follows. First I will motivate the subject and give references on already existing empirical works on this topic. Secondly, I will briefly summarize the methodology and state the sources. Finally, I will explain results with the help of graphics. Ultimately, I will discuss the empirical work. For brevity's sake, I will not elaborate profoundly on robustness checks, and not on regressions explained in the paper.

2.2.1 Methodology and Data Sources

The authors illustrate two models in which they analyze the impact of industrial robots and automation on employment and wages. The first model is a simplified version limited to a closed economy in which trade is restricted to the domestic market in one commuting zone[6]. This autarky model ignores the more realistic scenario in which regions interact with each other, as automation and subsequent reduction of production in one zone have a positive effect on the purchasing power and thereby employment of other zones.

---

[6]A commuting zone is a geographic area used in population and economic analysis. In addition to the major use of urban areas, it may be used to define rural areas which share a common market.

Hence, here I will review only the second and more realistic model – Open Economy – where trade zones, defined as Commuting Zones, can trade with each other.

The basis of the empirical work is about the competition between robots and workers in the production of different tasks. The impact of robots on wages and employment is estimated by regressing the change in the variables when exposed to robots in each industry. In concrete, Acemoglu looked at the sum over industries of the national penetration of robot times the baseline employment share of that industry in the labor market.

There are two periods from 1990-2000 and 2000-2007 observed in the following specification I review here. E1 regresses the change in Labor (L) in commuting zone $c \in C$ and the change in Wages (W) in commuting zone $c \in C$ while exposed to used robots for a given task.

$$\mathrm{dln}\, L_c = \beta_c^L \sum_{i \in I} \ell_{ci} \frac{\mathrm{d}R_i}{L_i} + \epsilon_c^L$$
$$\mathrm{dln}\, W_c = \beta_c^W \sum_{i \in I} \ell_{ci} \frac{\mathrm{d}R_i}{L_i} + \epsilon_c^W \tag{E1}$$

Both of the following coefficients are negative, where the elasticity of labor supply $(1/\epsilon)$, the elasticity of local labor supply (η), the physical productivity of labor relative to robots (γ), and the average cost savings from the introduction of robots $(\pi > 0)$ and trade elasticities λ and σ such that [7]

$$\beta_c^L \approx \left(\frac{1 + \eta}{1 + \varepsilon}(s_{cL}\lambda + (1 - c_{cL})\sigma)\pi_c - \frac{1 + \eta}{1 + \varepsilon} \frac{s_{cL}\lambda + 1 - s_{cL}}{s_{cL}} \right) \frac{v_c}{\gamma}$$
$$\beta_c^W \approx \left(\left((1 + \eta)\frac{(1 + \varepsilon)\lambda - 1}{1 + \varepsilon} - (1 + \eta(1 - s_{cL}))(\lambda - \sigma) \right)\pi_c - \tag{E2}$$
$$\left(\eta(\lambda - 1) + \frac{\varepsilon(1 + \eta)}{(1 + \varepsilon)s_{cL}} \right) \right) \frac{v_c}{\gamma},$$

where

$$v_c = \frac{(1 + \varepsilon)s_{cL}}{(1 + \varepsilon)s_{cL}\lambda + (1 + \eta)(1 - s_{cL})}.$$

The concerns about this empirical strategy are that the reason why robots are exposed in a given industry could be related to other trends affecting that industry or economic conditions. Additionally, the IFR industry-level data in the U.S. starts only in 2004, while in several European countries it already started in 1993. Thus, these two issues could expose the model to an Omitted Variable Bias. To solve this, the authors use Instrumental Variables. This approach enables the authors to estimate the impact of industrial robots over a more extended period. They use the industry-level spread of

---

[7] λ: Elasticity of substitution between varieties of the same good sourced from different commuting zones; σ: Elasticity of substitution between varieties of the same good sourced from different industries.

robots in other advanced economies[8] to proxy improvements in the robot technology as an instrument for the adoption of such technologies in the US.

The data from other advanced economies was extracted from the IFR (International Federation of Robotics) covering 50 countries from 1993 to 2014, which corresponds to 90% of the industrial robots market. However, detailed information about the industry breakdown is only delivered by Denmark, Finland, France, Germany, Italy, Norway, Spain, Sweden, and the UK, which make up 41% of the market. The latter mentioned advanced economies are used to proxy the spread of robots.

Additionally, the IFR only reports the overall stock of robots for North America. However, as the U.S. makes up 90% of the stock in North America, and Instrumental variables are used, this should not be a significant measurement error.

The IFR Data is combined with employment counts by country and industry in 1990 from the EUKLEMS dataset to measure the number of industrial robots per thousand workers by country, industry and time.

In the regression analysis, Acemoglu focuses on 722 commuting zones in the USA and extracts the data from public use data from the 1970 and 1990 Censuses to obtain the share of employment by industry. To construct measures of employment, employment by industry and occupation, and demographics for each commuting zones, they use the 2007 American Community Survey.

Moreover, the Censuses and American Community Survey are used to compute the average hourly and weekly wage within demographic times commuting zone cells, in order to estimate the effect of robots on comparable individuals.

Finally, they use data by Green Leigh and Kraft 2016 to obtain the locations and subsequently the number of companies that install and program robots.

2.2.2   Results

Before moving to the effects of automation on wages and employment, we will have a look at the aggregated figures of robot stocks in the USA and other parts of the world.

Figure 1 illustrates the evolution of the mean and 30th percentile of robot usage across the nine European economies mentioned in the previous section and average density of robot usage in the USA. The figure depicts the changing rates over time of robots per thousand workers in the USA and EU respectively. In the given European countries (USA), the robot usage starts near 0.6 (0.4) robots per thousand workers in the early 1990 and increases rapidly to 2.6 (1.4) robots in the late 2000s. In addition to these figures, we can also infer that the advanced European countries, do indeed follow the same trend as the U.S., and thus are in this respect a legitimate proxy for the Instrumental Variables.

Figure 2 plots the data on the use of robots in Europe for the set of industries covered in the IFR Data. Moreover, it reveals that those industries which have a higher normalized

---

[8]Denmark, Finland, France, Germany, Italy, Norway, Spain, Sweden, and the UK, which make up 41% of the world market.

Figure 1: Industrial robots in the United States and Europe.

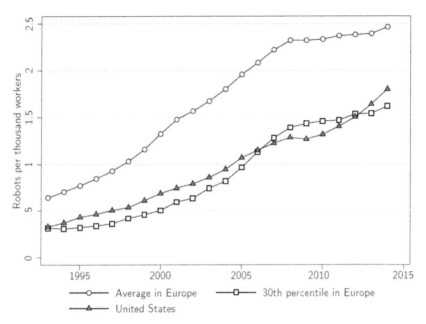

Source: Acemoglu and Restrepo (2017), Figure 1

figure for robot usages, don't have large figures for Chinese Imports per thousand workers, the percent increase in capital stock, and percent increase in IT capital stock. Which in turn highlights the robustness of the model stated here regarding error terms. Such that, the usage of robots is not majorly affected by other trends affecting the industries in developed countries.

Figure 3 exhibits different intensities of robot usage across all US commuting zones. Although automotive accounts for a high stake of robot usage as can be seen in 2, when excluding automobile manufacturing, the panel still explains 68% of the original variation. Also, even though manufacturing industries claim 80% of the industrial robots usage, the share of manufacturing employment explains only about 18 percent of the variation in exposure to robots across commuting zones. The variation in the commuting zones arises from the different mix of industries in those locations. Additionally, in 3 Panels C-F depicts the consistency that the geographic distribution of exposure to robots in Panel A-B is not conspicuously congruent with the geographic distribution of exposure to Chinese imports, exposure to Mexican imports, routine jobs and offshoring.

These figures highlight not only the accuracy of the proxy but also that this model is very robust to exogenous factors which potentially could have biased the outcomes.

Figure 2: Industry-level changes in the use of robots, Chinese imports, capital stock and IT capital.

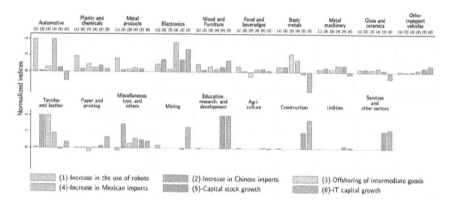

Source: Acemoglu and Restrepo (2017), Figure 2

Descriptive Statistics: Table 2 in the Appendix provides basic descriptive statistics. The quartiles show the intensity of the exposure to robots. It indicates that with a higher quartile, automation should have more intense effects on employment and wages[9]. Initially, if we compare the private employment to population ratio in Panel A, column 1 and 2 and the hourly wages in 1990 in column 7 we see that the effect of automation in all four quartiles are very similar. However, regarding the change of employment and wages in column 2-6 and 8-9 respectively, we see with higher Quartiles an increasingly negative effect of robots.

Panel B provides information for the right-hand side of the regression. We can see that by increasing quartiles, the share of employment in manufacturing increases as well. However, this is not surprising as exposure to robots was relatively small in non-manufacturing industries. Moreover, the panel reveals similarly to the results in figure 3, that there is a small correlation between the exposure to robots and Chinese imports, Mexican imports, the share of routine jobs and offshoring. Nevertheless, these figures are included in this regression model.

The impact on Employment and Wages: Table 1 plots the regression of E1 and E2 for 1990-2000 and 2000-2007 and exhibits very significant results. Panel A to D state significant negative effects of robots on employment and wages respectively at the 1% level for all controlled specifications. Panel A and B illustrate the effect of robots on employment. The Census data, Panel A, measures employment from the household side, while the CBP data, Panel B, approaches it from the employer side, making the two datasets complementary. Moreover, Panel C and D measure the effect of robots on Log

---

[9]see Table 3 for this.

14

Figure 3: Geographic distribution of the exposure to robots, the exposure to Chinese imports, Mexican imports, routine jobs, and the exposure to offshoring.

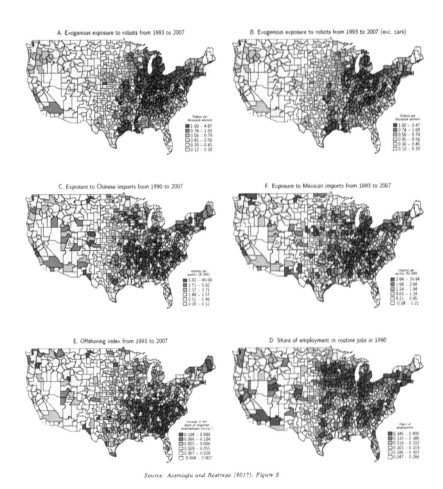

A. Exogenous exposure to robots from 1993 to 2007

B. Exogenous exposure to robots from 1993 to 2007 (exc. cars)

C. Exposure to Chinese imports from 1990 to 2007

F. Exposure to Mexican imports from 1993 to 2007

E. Offshoring index from 1993 to 2007

D. Share of employment in routine jobs in 1990

hourly wage and Log weekly wage respectively.

The results suggest a strong negative relationship between commuting zone's exposure to robots and both employment and wages. When controlling for exogenous variations, in aggregate one additional robot between 1993 and 2007 reduced the employment by 3-5.6 workers and an additional robot per thousand workers reduced wages in the US by 0.25 percent to 0.5 percent. If only industries most exposed to robots are observed, the negative impact remains, though the effect reduces to 3 workers and 0.25%. Interestingly similar, when removing areas with high exposure to robots in Table 1, all results, albeit

Table 1: The impact of the exposure to robots on employment and wages
(stacked differences)

STACKED-DIFFERENCES ESTIMATES 1990-2000 AND 2000-2007

	(1)	(2)	(3)	(4)	(5)	(6)
	Panel A. Census private employment to population ratio.					
Exposure to robots	-0.951***	-0.953***	-1.384***	-1.346***	-1.249***	-0.613***
	(0.152)	(0.146)	(0.174)	(0.139)	(0.339)	(0.111)
Observations	1444	1444	1444	1441	1427	1444
	Panel B. CBP employment to population ratio.					
Exposure to robots	-1.891***	-1.958***	-1.877***	-1.695***	-2.459***	-1.922***
	(0.300)	(0.310)	(0.256)	(0.209)	(0.674)	(0.379)
Observations	1444	1444	1444	1436	1427	1444
	Panel C. Log hourly wage.					
Exposure to robots	-1.939***	-1.919***	-2.176***	-1.485***	-2.428**	-2.519***
	(0.342)	(0.375)	(0.513)	(0.436)	(0.918)	(0.489)
Observations	326377	326377	326377	318420	321643	326377
	Panel D. Log weekly wage.					
Exposure to robots	-3.266***	-3.200***	-3.979***	-2.471***	-4.117***	-3.734***
	(0.399)	(0.434)	(0.609)	(0.457)	(1.084)	(0.764)
Observations	326377	326377	326377	317850	321643	326377
Covariates & sample restrictions:						
Demographic, industry shares and census division dummies	✓	✓	✓	✓	✓	✓
Trade, routinization and offshoring		✓	✓	✓	✓	✓
Unweighted			✓			
Down-weights outliers				✓		
Removes highly exposed areas					✓	
Commuting zone fixed effects						✓

Source: Acemoglu and Restrepo (2017) Table 3

Panel A less, exhibit stronger negative results. The reason for the latter results could be, that highly exposed areas already have introduced AI friendly policies to transform the economy to a balanced growth path.

According to Figure A1 in the Appendix, we can infer that regarding occupation employment, robots highest negative effect is on routine manual and blue-collar workers, with each reaching almost -6% of displacement. In Contrast, Services, Management, and Financiers are barely negatively affected by robots.

The colored columns in A1 and A3 are distinguished as follows. Green columns indicate results of long-differences. These include only one observing change per commuting zone in the regression. The red columns are confined to the non-extreme values which affect the results immensely. Finally, the blue columns include two observations per commuting zone in one ten year period.

2.2.3 Discussion

These results seem to follow a trend in which robots can automate tasks which are confined to only a small scope of decision-making. In the same way, automation is taking place in tasks which require motor skills. Thus, mostly the blue-collar workforce in routine manual tasks could be affected. Also, on the other hand, robots seem not to be able to automate tasks which require a lot of decision-making and brainwork rather than routine work – thus tasks in Management and Finance. Moreover, as there is no evidence suggesting that Artificial Intelligence has emotions, one could infer that future human capital could experience a remarkable shift of skill sets towards emotional resilience and decision-making Yuval Harari Interview (2017).

The distinction between Long-Differences, Downweight Outliers, and Stacked Differences is crucial to understand long-term developments in each occupation or industry. While the green columns exhibit vague results based on the average effect in the period between 1993 and 2007, the blue columns reveal more accurate results by averaging weighted effects in each 10-year period. As a result, one can suggest that blue columns are outlining constant changes within an occupation. An illustrative example can be found in Figure A1 when elaborating on Farmers and Miners. While the green column only reveals small negative effects, the blue column reveals much higher negative effects, suggesting that over time, e.g., by technological improvements in the years 2000-2007, the displacement effect was much higher. This is intuitive if we assume that inventing new technologies has accelerated faster in the second period than in the first, 1990-2000. Indeed, U.S. Patent and Trademark Office (USPTO) (2015), state that Utility Patents inventions between 1990-2000 were on average 115,080 while between 2000-2007 the figure goes up to 143,896, which is 25% higher. Furthermore, if we carefully analyze the red column, one can easily see that it reveal the highest negative effects on occupation employment and wages respectively. This could be explained by regulatory reasons, such that, if we exert extreme values, the vacancies which are for example protected by law, one could suggest that this reveals the actual effect of robots. This becomes clear in Figure A1 for occupation employments in Routine Manual and Blue-Collar, where the Older Workers Benefit Protection Act (OWBPA) protects many workers.

Furthermore, in Figure A2 in the Appendix, it is counterintuitive to see that education profiles with "Less than highschool" exhibit approximately the least negative employment effects while "Highschool," "Some college," and "College" reveal 0.5, 0.8 and 0.8 percentage points more negative employment effects. This could be explained by the dismissal protection – Older Workers Benefit Protection (OWBPA) - for workers over 40 without any higher education working in the industry. This argument is even stronger if we moreover assume that higher education was not as prevalent as it is today. So, elder people with less education are protected, but younger people with more education are not. All in all, this could lead to an Omitted Variable Bias, namely the dismissal protection for workers over 40.

17

Similarly counterintuitive, looking at the hourly wage effects in Figure A2, it is surprising that there are no positive effects on wages in any education groups, albeit the higher education profiles exhibit less of a wage decline. The reason for that could arise from uncertain prospects about future substituted tasks on which the wages are calculated, such that one can suggest that a task is abolished but not with which new task it will be replaced.

Moreover, Figure A3 in the Appendix depicts the Exposure to robots and its effect on wage distributions. The figure shows the estimates of change in the 10th to 90th wage deciles. It becomes evident that lower wage distributions are tremendously negatively affected by the exposure to robots. Whereas the 80th and 90th percentile exhibit even positive effects when measured by long-differences. This is intuitive if we compare the increased GINI Index of the USA from 1994[10] to 2007 with 40.2 and 41.1 respectively and thereby assume that on average over the whole period, the wage inequality increased. Though not a strong evidence, one could argue that at least the GINI coefficient does not oppose the hypothesis.

3 Policymaking

In this section, I am reviewing Cath et al. (2018) to compare the policies based on the following three topics:

- The Development of a "good AI society"

- The role and responsibility of the government, the private sector, and the research community in pursuing such a development

- Whether the recommendations to support such a development may be in need of improvement

Generally, the reports seem to have an all-enhancing consideration of AI, however, fail to develop an explicit vision of the role that AI should play in "mature information societies." The term 'Mature information societies' relates to the importance of addressing current ethical challenges that AI poses. As their reliance on AI increase, the impact of AI technologies on our shared values will increase.

Ironically, however, the more AI technologies advance in complexity, the more intangible it becomes for the society. As a consequence, the impact on the society can't be easily grasped. This is why governments must make socio-political decisions to set up a framework. Otherwise, the private sector or academia could fill the vacuum by setting up mere standards, leaving the legal framework insecure.

---

[10]Although this regression starts with the year 1993, due to no consistent available data, I assume that between 1993 and 1994 the Coefficient did not change drastically. This is supported by the low variance of the GINI index.

Additionally, the frictionless adjustment of incentives of only the private sector and academia to the social needs seems somewhat doubtful. The other way around, the incentives of a state as a leading social planner must collaborate with the incentives of the other two stakeholders, thus receive information about the incentives of companies and academia. Otherwise, innovations in the AI technology could be decelerated by uncertain hesitating states.

This paper concludes that the best future of a "good AI society" is one in which it helps the infosphere and the biosphere to prosper together.

This section is structured as follows. The first subsection will review the U.S. approach of AI-related policymaking. Afterward, I will discuss the implications of the aimed policies and suggest novel research on the next section.

3.1 The U.S. approach

After comparing the three approaches, I came to the conclusion that the US report distinguishes from the other two reports concerning scope and depth. Therefore, to have an all-enclosing perspective of notions about AI related policy making, I decided to focus on the US policy strategies. After stating a brief overview of what the U.S. government published so far, I will focus on the policies specially made to mitigate the adverse employment and wage effects of AI described in previous sections.

The U.S. report on AI, entitled 'Preparing for the Future of Artificial Intelligence' was released on October 12th, 2016 by the Executive Office of the President National Science and Technology Council Committee on Technology (2016). The report followed five public workshops and an official Request for Information on AI[11].

According to this report, the government sees its role in managing the tasks of defining the framework for what AI should be used for and for collecting data to inform policymaking. However, the government does not intend to prevent the private sector from liberally innovating AI, albeit within the confines of the broad risk management regulatory framework. The report emphasizes the importance of the collaboration between the research community, industry, and government in ensuring that AI is accountable, transparent and its operation will remain consistent with "human values and aspirations."

The above-mentioned "human values and aspirations" are not closely defined, hence there is no notion about how to achieve socially acceptable policies for the development of AI. However, there is another document by the National Science and Technology Council (2016)[12] titled "The National Artificial Intelligence Research and Development Strategic Plan" which does provide a more detailed outline in which areas R&D investments related to AI should be used.

The report is classified into divisions like Cross-cutting R&D Foundations which are essential for all AI research. These divisions break down to subdivisions called Basic

---

[11]A Request for Information is a draft bill by experts addressed to the president.
[12]The US President's entourage in technology-related topics.

R&D such as Long-Term Investments or Human-AI Collaboration. At the bottom is the sub-subdivision called Applications. Each division covers topics such as Ethical-Legal and Societal Implications, Human Augmentation, and specific application like Education.

Figure 4: Organization of the AI RD Strategic Plan.

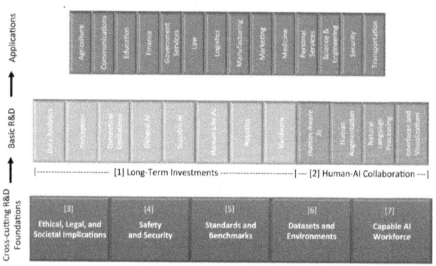

The goal of this strategic plan is to understand how to define and advance policies that ensure the responsible, safe, and beneficial use of AI, by focusing on the significant R&D investments.

Finally, the Executive Office of the President (2016) also addresses specifically the sensitive ambiguous effect of AI making jobs redundant and creating new jobs by publishing a report titled "Artificial Intelligence, Automation and the Economy" in collaboration with a team from the White House Executive Office of the President, which I will review in the next section.

3.2 Policy Responses to AI and its Effect on Employment and Wages

The report of the Executive Office of the President (2016) highlights the impact of AI-driven automation on the US job market and economy. Three specific policy responses are presented as follows.

1. Invest in and develop AI for its many benefits

The report claims that diversity in race and gender is crucial to the development of innovative technologies. An intuitive reason Gebru (2011)[13] considers is that AI affects a variety of issues in the society, and while developing and regulating these technologies, only a diverse background of the stakeholder, thus researchers and policymakers, can be reasonably able to find the answers. For instance, Big Data [14] which is based on substantial up-to-date datasets can train AI to spot clear patterns for specific job descriptions. While enabling the Human Resources Management to find the better fit for the specific job, looking at the current non-heterogenic workforce, it is predestined that the underrepresented genders and races will inherently be discriminated and potential talent excluded. This development is very probable, considering not only the actual current discrimination in the job market but more importantly, how this resembles in the data sets. This is why this report suggests the government to regulate future job markets.

Finally, the report recommends the government to not only invest in the research in STEM[15] fields who technically develop AI, but equally important, also in entrepreneurship, economics, social science, and health. Moreover, it encourages the gender and racial equality.

2. Educate and train Americans for the jobs of the future

Assuming the accuracy of my critics regarding Figure A2 in Section 2.2.3 about the statistical bias in Figure 12, one can infer that higher education prevents losing jobs and wages.

The second point emphasizes the importance of the early childhood education. A lack of basic skills in maths and reading make it harder to catch up in the future as Juel (1988) suggests. American students still struggle to catch up with their international peers in mathematics as stated by OECD (2012). This is relevant considering the prospects, that skill sets will evolve at a faster rate. Hence, having the basic skills could enable students to retrain at a faster pace.

Additionally, the former president of the U.S. Barack Obama founded the *Computer Science for All* initiative, which allows K12 level students[16] to have access to coursework in computing and computational thinking. The initiative is supported in a collaboration of governors, mayors, and other public- and private-sector leaders who help to create new standards, courses, and investments.

---

[13]Founder of the company Black in AI.
[14]Big Data supplies Artificial Intelligence with massive data sets and can organize them.
[15]Science, Technology, Engineering, and Mathematics.
[16]K-12, a term used in education and educational technology in the United States, Canada, and possibly other countries, is a short form for the publicly-supported school grades prior to college. These grades are kindergarten (K) and the 1st through the 12th grade (1-12).

3. Aid workers in the transition and empower workers to ensure broadly shared growth

As concluded in Section 2.1.5 the transition process towards a society in which AI can enable a balanced growth path could prove to be a challenging task. As new technologies disrupt business models and thereby change the set of skills needed for solving new problems, continuous learning and adapting becomes the standard. Even more so, when considering AI's implication on many not so trivial areas (e.g., Smelter Operators, Oil Refineries, and Regtechs - Boston Consulting Group (2017)). Another impeding effect is regulatory measures which secure on the one hand a secure launch of technologies, but on the other hand, could hamper innovation.

To provide an overview, I will elaborate on three measures which I found to be fostering a smooth transition period:

1. *Financial Aids*

   As a response to the expected displacements in the labor market, the report highlights the importance of a safety net. That is to say, enhancing unemployment insurance, Medicaid, Supplemental Nutrition Assistance Program (SNAP), and Temporary Assistance for Needy Families (TANF)[17].

   Expanding the unemployment insurance by wage insurance could enormously benefit experienced workers who after changing their jobs end up earning on average 10% less than in the previous job.

   Moreover, with the rise of high staff-turnover and part-time jobs, it is crucial to ensure that workers can access retirement, health care, and other benefits, whether or not they receive them on the job.

   Although the authors do not specify, in the face of unprecedented disruption, they recommend an improved safety net which goes beyond the conventional aid.

2. *Advising employees on education and training and access to labor-market information*

   Jacobson and Petta (2000) have shown that relatively affordable job-search assistance programs speeded up employment by one to two weeks.

3. *Labor-market regulation and enhancing working conditions*

   Finally, the report raises the trend of increasing Labor Market Monopsony published by The Council of Economic Advisers (2016)). In the light of shifting powers towards employers by ever-increasing capital accumulation, as mentioned in Section 2.1.1, high-tech giants could be inclined to entrench their powers to the detriment of

---

[17]Redistributing measures. SNAP, e.g., Food Stamps and TANF, e.g., cash assistance.

workers. To eliminate this threat, the report recommends enhancing the regulation of wages, competition, and worker bargaining power.

Labor unions have exemplified how workers can collectively enforce the protection of their rights. So, it is recommended that in the future, governments should enable labor unions to strengthen their position in order to counterweight the increasing power of employers.

Moreover, raising the minimum wage is often treated very cautiously, and with good reason, by economic advisors. However, considering that Dube (2013) suggests that the value of the minimum wage in the U.S. has fallen by nearly a quarter from its peak value in 1968, the report concludes that now would be an appropriate time to raise the minimum wages.

Ultimately, another trend is the continuing urbanization and thus concentrated human capital in big cities which at the end stand at the forefront of working towards AI. People living in rural areas, on the other hand, lack the opportunity to work in such metropolises because of increasing housing prices due to higher demand. Also, rural areas have only limited access to broadband and public transit. Removing such barriers could improve the conditions for a more significant share of the society.

3.3 Discussion

Besides the basic education, a crucial topic to enable the workforce is by training and re-training for specific jobs. Even though one could think that training for a specific job would be enough to execute a particular set of tasks, the prospects instead suggest that re-training will be inherently necessary in order to align to the ever-changing disruption in technology and hence job descriptions. Such trends can already be observed in the U.S. as Figure 5 depicts.

Between 1970 and 2015 the number of college students enrolled in Fall aged 25 and older increased nearly fourfold, whereas the number of college students younger than 25 increased only twofold. Though the data does not specify in repeated college education, one can still infer that older people more and more go back to university to train or re-train themselves.

However, the U.S. public spending to support these training measures has shrunk to its half compared to 30 years ago (see Figure A4), amounting to 0.1%, whereas on average, OECD[18] countries spend 0.6% as illustrated by Figure A3. The report of the Executive Office of the President (2016), rightly in my view, recommends a sixfold increase in public spending for job training programs, which would retrain 2.5 million people per year[19].

Such programs become in the face of AI ever more critical as needed education and training is from today's perspective relatively opaque. However, the other way around,

---

[18]An organization of rich countries

[19]This assumes $6,000 per person training/reemployment cost, and an increase in Workforce Innovation and Opportunity Act funding from today's $3B to $18B with all new funding spent on training.

Figure 5: Enrollment in degree-granting postsecondary institutions, by age: Fall 1970 through fall 2026.

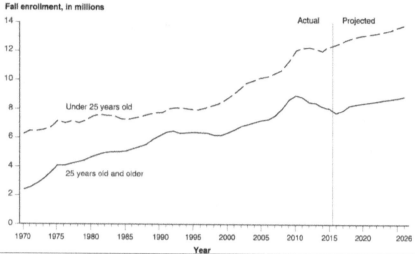

Source: U.S. Department of Education, National Center for Education Statistics, Higher Education General Information Survey (HEGIS), Figure 14

Figure 6: Public Expenditure on Active Labor Market Programs (% of GDP)

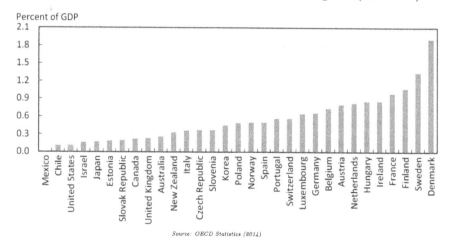

Source: OECD Statistics (2014)

AI can positively contribute to the matching of talents and jobs. For instance, a French startup Riminder has developed a deep learning-powered platform to compare applicant resumes with an organization's current employees as well as other people in the world with similar job titles. So, recruiters can view a candidate's strengths and weaknesses. Public spending could be conditioned to such job-finding guidances in collaboration with StartUps or other corporations.

Hence, until we figure out how to adapt to the new way of continuous learning, there has to be established firm intermediate stages. These stages should not be confused with potential lean-back solutions like Universal Basic Income (UBI[20]) but rather as a reactivating safety net. The danger arising from UBI, in my and the report's author's opinion, is that it gives up on reinstating the displaced workforce.

One of the implications of such universal measures is that if we decide that some people become economically obsolete, albeit agitating as a consumer, this could raise the inequality much higher than it currently is. UBI does not prevent parents from being uneducated and acting as a negative multiplier to their children. The immediate impact the children have is not only the poor education but also the absence of prospects for a good education, hence leaving them underprivileged. Sure, there are supportive voices raised to consider UBI as a redistribution by wealthy individuals as a response to disrupting Artificial Intelligence, like recently from Obama in the 16th Nelson Mandela Annual Lecture in Johannesburg. However, before we reach to such controversial measures, we should exploit measures which have proven to be supportive of major societal transformations.

A better interpretation of the intermediate stages is, in my opinion, a supporting, discriminatory income which is bound by rules. Thus, rather than arbitrary distribution, there should be concentrated efforts to support self-help resourcefulness. One way to do this could be to encourage institutions who discuss and redirect research topics about AI, like Partnership on AI[21], to voluntarily contribute to a fund. In collaboration with the U.S. government, this fund could be used to finance special training and re-training programs for especially the younger generations apart from the public spending on labor-market regulatory and advisory measures. One option in concrete could be that benevolent companies make an effort to re-train not only their employees but rather in a collective manner, all displaced workers in AI-related fields. The government could incentivize such endeavors with tax breaks for companies as well as for workers.

Moreover, all three reports state that there needs to be more openly accessible and unbiased datasets, privacy considerations, and ethical training for engineers. However, it also states that the moral education of the public is just as important. Also, this paper claims that the decision makers leave the question of authority and legitimacy open by not assigning the liabilities. I object to this opinion based on my conviction that the public takes a decisive role in forming AI implications just as much as the other stakeholders. Thus, the public should be semi-sovereign in her knowledge regarding the AI implications to adjust themselves. Hence, the government is responsible for providing the sources to educate oneself, but the public must help themselves.

Ultimately, The Partnership on AI to Benefit People and Society is a promising institution, yet inclined towards false incentives. It is a collaborative organization of the research community, the private sector and other non-profit organization which aims to research on the use of AI, shape best practices and foster public dialogue about AI's

---

[20] An unreserved and indiscriminate basic income for every humanbeing.
[21] An Association of tech-giants and academics based in San Francisco.

benefits for people and society. Although the Partnership on AI denies being a Lobbying Organization, it is legitimate to ask oneself whether the endeavors could be biased towards the interests of the for-profit companies - GAFA[22] among other - which after all finance the organization.

4 Further novel research

Ultimately, I will state four crucial issues which are essential to fully understand the impact of Artificial Intelligence and automation on the society.

First, in Section 2.1.1, I reviewed the Productivity gains from AI and its counterbalancing effect against the aggregated displacement effect. This counterbalancing effect, though, depends on increasing demand for products. Along with this, in the same section, I also mentioned that increasing automation causes increased inequality by lowering the share of labor in national income. If, as a consequence of this distributional shifting, the higher national income ends up in a smaller share of the population with much lower marginal tendency[23] to consume, the counterbalancing force could be weakened. In order to understand whether countervailing effects function, one should study empirically how much AI affects inequality and thereby the consumption.

Second, in Section 2.2.3 I highlighted how the mismatch of new skills could impede the transition towards an AI integrated society. Hence, rather than investing more at random in education, there has to be studied in specific how a new education could look like. Acemoglu and Restrepo (2018) illustrate this by highlighting that "[...] AI and other new automation technologies necessitate a mix of numeracy, communication, and problem-solving skills different than those emphasized in current curricula [...]".

Third, in Section 2.1.5 I concluded that there is a conflict of interest between excessively investing in AI and accelerating the acquisition of new skills. Governments profoundly affect how much investments are done in AI and how the population is educated. This they do directly by tax incentives for investments and regulations and various policies regarding the education system. The research on the impact of these policies including social factors is crucial on the path of development of AI.

Finally, one should not take the adoption and development of new technologies for granted. Indeed, in Section 3 Policy Making, I underlined how crucial it is that we find a way of shared prosperity whilst integrating AI into our society. Otherwise, there is the risk that decision makers slow down the adoption or even stop the development of such technologies.

---

[22]Big Four tech companies: Google, Amazon, Facebook and Apple.
[23]Marginal propensity to consume (MPC) decreases in disposable incomes.

5 Conclusion

Acemoglu suggests that the false dichotomy arising in the topic of AI is due to a lack of adequate conceptual framework. To solve this, Acemoglu and Restrepo (2018) propose a conceptual framework which emphasizes the task-based approach in which automation replaces labor in tasks which it used to perform. This causes a displacement effect. If not counterbalanced, it will reduce labor demand, wages and consequently employment. However, there are countervailing effects like the Productivity Effect, Capital Accumulation, Deepening of automation.

All in all, there is always a displacement effect on labor resulting from automation[24]. However, the productivity effect could outweigh the displacement effect. In contrast to the widespread fear, not the super-productive technologies threaten the labor, but the "so-so" ones, because they are not productive enough.

In addition to that, automation will always reduce the share of labor in national income, even with the countervailing effects of capital accumulation and deepening of automation. However, this could be counterbalanced by new tasks in which labor has a comparative advantage; thus the demand for labor could grow with productivity at par, which tended to be the case in the past.

However, today empirical data suggests that displacements happen far more than we have seen in the last decades[25]. This trend challenges the conventional aids provided by governments. For instance, if the share of labor in national income continuously decreases, which it would as a consequence of displacement, but the workforce in numbers does not, the redistribution through the tax system could take some serious hits. If we add my theory that older workers with less education[26], which are secured by protection laws, positively bias the adverse effects of automation, we could be facing a much higher rate of displacement than initially assumed.

With all these unprecedented potential waves of disruptions caused by AI, the government is required to deal intensively with AI regulation to ensure both innovation and beneficial regulation.

The EU helpfully recommends the creation of "European Agency for Robotics and AI," which shall monitor not only current developments in the field of AI but also advise public players on the future impact and vision. Furthermore, the report makes a lot of useful recommendations regarding the light-handed regulation for the sake of not hampering innovation, hence surprisingly similar to US policies.

The UK report relies on existing and new regulatory frameworks in dealing with AI's implications on society. It is, in fact, the only report recommending an independent standing by creating a national Commission which organizes public debates about the challenges arising from AI.

---

[24]see T5.
[25]see Section 2.2.3.
[26]see Section 2.2.3.

However, all reports lack the clear outlining of a long-term strategy and political vision for the development of a good AI society. Probably because from today's point of view, it seems somewhat contestable.

All in all, the US OSTP report on AI raised the awareness of the necessity of publicly debating about the topic, which yet cannot be said of the EU and UK reports. Moreover, the US report is unique in elaborating on Research and Development strategies by including the work of experts and the public by public workshops and government by the "Request of Information."

References

Accenture PLC. "How Companies Are Reimagining Business Processes With IT".

D. Acemoglu and P. Restrepo. "The Race Between Machine and Man: Implications of Technology for Growth, Factor Shares and Employment". NBER Working Paper No. 22252, 2016.

D. Acemoglu and P. Restrepo. "Robots and Jobs: Evidence from US Labor Markets". NBER Working Paper No. w23285, 2017.

D. Acemoglu and P. Restrepo. "Artificial Intelligence, Automation and Work". NBER Working Paper No. 24196, 2018.

R. C. Allen. "Engels' pause: Technical change, capital accumulation, and inequality in the british industrial revolution". Explorations in Economic History, 46(4):418–435, 2009.

D. H. Autor, F. Levy, and R. J. Murnane. "The skill content of recent technological change: An empirical exploration". The Quarterly journal of economics, 118(4):1279–1333, 2003.

J. Bessen. "Learning by doing: the real connection between innovation, wages, and wealth", volume 287. Yale University Press, 2015.

Boston Consulting Group. "The Robotics Revolution: The Next Great Leap in Manufacturing". 2015.

Boston Consulting Group. "Putting Artificial Intelligence to Work". 2017.

E. Brynjolfsson and A. McAfee. "The second machine age: Work, progress, and prosperity in a time of brilliant technologies", volume 295. WW Norton & Company, 2014.

C. Cath, S. Wachter, B. Mittelstadt, M. Taddeo, and L. Floridi. "Artificial Intelligence and the 'Good Society': the US, EU, and UK approach". Science and Engineering Ethics, 24(2):505–528, 2018.

Deloitte. "Boiling Point? The Skills Gap in U.S. Manufacturing".

A. Dube. Minimum wages and the distribution of family incomes. A Paper Series Commemorating the 75 th Anniversary of the Fair Labor Standards Act, page 172, 2013.

Executive Office of the President. "Artificial Intelligence, Automation and the Economy". 2016.

Executive Office of the President National Science and Technology Council Committee on Technology. "Preparing for the future of artificial intelligence". 2016.

C. B. Frey and M. A. Osborne. "The future of employment: how susceptible are jobs to computerisation?" Technological forecasting and social change, 114:254–280, 2017.

T. Gebru. "We're in a diversity crisis", 2011. URL https://www.technologyreview.com/s/610192/were-in-a-diversity-crisis-black-in-ais-founder-on-whats-poisoning-the-algorithms-in-our/.

M. Goos and A. Manning. "Lousy and lovely jobs: The rising polarization of work in Britain". The review of economics and statistics, 89(1):118–133, 2007.

G. Graetz and G. Michaels. "Robots at work". CEPR Discussion Paper No. DP10477, 2015.

Y. N. Harari. "Reboot for the AI revolution". Nature News, 550, 2017.

B. Herrendorf, R. Rogerson, and A. Valentinyi. "Two perspectives on preferences and structural transformation". American Economic Review, 103(7):2752–89, 2013.

L. Jacobson and I. Petta. "Measuring the Effect of Public Labor Exchange (PLX) Referrals and Placements in Washington and Oregon". OWS Occasional Paper, 6, 2000.

C. Juel. "Learning to read and write: A longitudinal study of 54 children from first through fourth grades". Journal of educational Psychology, 80(4):437, 1988.

R. E. Manuelli and A. Seshadri. "Frictionless technology diffusion: The case of tractors". American Economic Review, 104(4):1368–91, 2014.

McKinsey. "Jobs Lost, Jobs Gained: Workforce Transitions in a Time of Automation". 2017.

G. Michaels, A. Natraj, and J. Van Reenen. "Has ICT polarized skill demand? Evidence from eleven countries over twenty-five years". Review of Economics and Statistics, 96 (1):60–77, 2014.

National Science and Technology Council. "The National Artificial Intelligence Research and Development Strategic Plan". 2016.

OECD. "Program for International Student Assessment 2012 Results", 2012. URL https://www.oecd.org/unitedstates/PISA-2012-results-US.pdf.

A. L. Olmstead and P. W. Rhode. "Reshaping the landscape: the impact and diffusion of the tractor in American agriculture, 1910–1960". The Journal of Economic History, 61 (3):663–698, 2001.

The Council of Economic Advisers. "Issue Brief: Labor Market Monopsony: Trends, Consequences, and Policy Responses". 2016. Retrieved from https://www.whitehouse.gov/sites/default/files/page/files/20161025_monopsony_labor_mrkt_c

S. Thrun and L. Pratt. "Learning to learn", volume 353. Springer Science & Business Media, 2012.

U.S. Patent and Trademark Office (USPTO). "Table of Annual U.S. Patent Activity Since 1790", 2015. URL https://www.uspto.gov/web/offices/ac/ido/oeip/taf/h_counts.htm.

R. Werning. "Stichwort: Schulische Inklusion". Zeitschrift für Erziehungswissenschaft, 17 (4):601–623, 2014.

Yuval Harari Interview. "How Humankind Could Become Totally Useless", 2017. URL http://time.com/4672373/yuval-noah-harari-homo-deus-interview/.

6 Appendix

6.1 Table and Figures

Table 2: Summary statistics.

	ALL ZONES $N = 722$	Q1 $N = 304$	Q2 $N = 202$	Q3 $N = 129$	Q4 $N = 87$
			QUARTILES OF THE CHANGE IN EXPOSURE TO ROBOTS		
			Panel A. Outcomes		
Census private employment to population ratio in 1990	0.354 [0.044]	0.317 [0.039]	0.357 [0.049]	0.363 [0.035]	0.376 [0.029]
CBP employment to population ratio in 1990	0.381 [0.074]	0.336 [0.070]	0.390 [0.084]	0.389 [0.063]	0.408 [0.057]
Change in Census private employment to population ratio from 1990 to 2007 (in p.p.)	0.294 [2.240]	1.486 [2.336]	0.418 [2.271]	-0.599 [2.208]	-0.117 [1.564]
Change in CBP employment to population ratio from 1990 to 2007 (in p.p.)	2.002 [3.791]	3.627 [4.880]	2.592 [3.275]	0.740 [3.547]	1.074 [2.419]
Change of Census log employment from 1990 to 2007 (in p.p.)	18.688 [14.838]	27.132 [16.894]	21.978 [15.213]	15.191 [11.001]	10.844 [9.613]
Change of CBP log employment from 1990 to 2007 (in p.p.)	23.208 [17.439]	32.942 [21.023]	27.559 [16.549]	18.919 [13.146]	13.857 [10.871]
Hourly wages in 1990	15.609 [2.493]	15.493 [3.055]	14.979 [2.364]	15.862 [2.337]	16.096 [2.004]
Change in the log of hourly wages from 1990 to 2007 (in p.p.), adjusted for composition	-3.844 [4.552]	-1.803 [5.354]	-1.871 [4.381]	-5.397 [3.241]	-6.236 [2.969]
Change in the log of weekly wages from 1990 to 2007 (in p.p.), adjusted for composition	-5.252 [5.210]	-2.047 [5.456]	-3.480 [4.885]	-7.236 [3.791]	-8.135 [3.922]
			Panel B. Covariates		
Share of employment in manufacturing 1990	0.225 [0.079]	0.150 [0.053]	0.233 [0.073]	0.252 [0.073]	0.262 [0.062]
Share of employment in durables 1990	0.136 [0.059]	0.085 [0.036]	0.135 [0.044]	0.153 [0.049]	0.167 [0.066]
Exposure to Chinese imports from 1990 to 2007	3.363 [2.059]	2.229 [1.296]	3.667 [2.205]	4.165 [2.322]	3.392 [1.782]
Share of employment in routine jobs 1990	0.346 [0.026]	0.339 [0.032]	0.340 [0.025]	0.347 [0.020]	0.357 [0.020]
Exposure to offshoring from 1993 to 2007	0.073 [0.083]	0.048 [0.061]	0.082 [0.095]	0.094 [0.103]	0.068 [0.059]
Exposure to Mexican imports from 1991 to 2007	1.863 [1.731]	1.005 [0.850]	1.756 [1.821]	1.958 [1.012]	2.678 [2.304]
Share of working-age population in 1990	0.658 [0.025]	0.651 [0.035]	0.659 [0.027]	0.663 [0.020]	0.658 [0.015]
Share of population with college in 1990	0.193 [0.056]	0.196 [0.063]	0.200 [0.064]	0.187 [0.050]	0.190 [0.047]

Source. Acemoglu and Restrepo (2017), Table 1

Figure A1: Relationship between the exposure to robots and occupation employment.

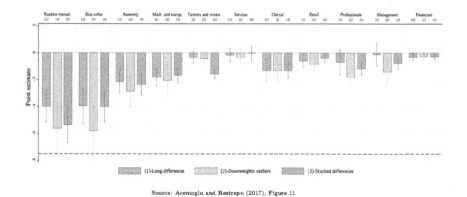

Source: Acemoglu and Restrepo (2017), Figure 11

Figure A2: Relationship between the exposure to robots and employment and wages by education group.

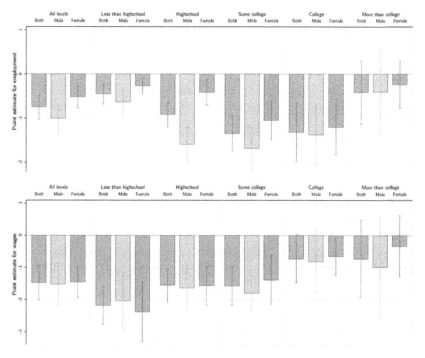

Source: Acemoglu and Restrepo (2017), Figure 12

Figure A3: Relationship between the exposure to robots and the wage distribution.

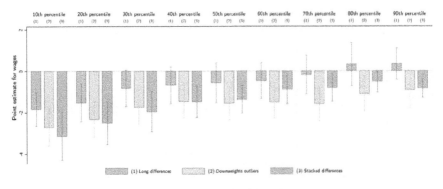

Source: Acemoglu and Restrepo (2017), Figure 13

Figure A4: U.S. Public Expenditure on Active Labor Market Programs Over Time as Percent of GDP

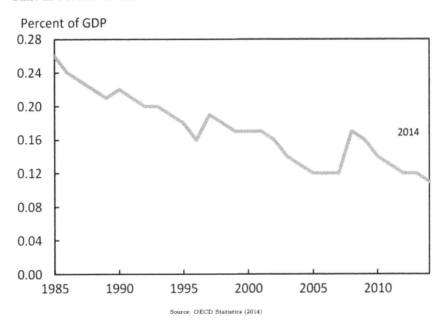

Source: OECD Statistics (2014)